11+
Verbal Activity
Verbal Reasoning Technique

WORKBOOK 1

Dr Stephen C Curran
with Jacqui Turner

Edited by Andrea Richardson and Katrina MacKay

This book belongs to

Krissh

Accelerated Education Publications Ltd.

Contents

1. Alphabet Reasoning
Pages
1. Letter Sequencing — 3-7
2. Alphabet Codes — 8-16

2. Word Patterns and Codes
1. Word Patterns — 17-21
2. Secret Code — 21-23
3. Mixed Examples — 23

3. Vocabulary with Spelling
1. Letter Shift — 24-25
2. Compound Word — 25-27
3. Hidden Word — 28-29
4. Missing Letter — 29-30
5. Mixed Examples — 31

4. Vocabulary with Meaning
1. Analogy — 32-33
2. Similar Meanings — 34-35
3. Word Link — 35-37
4. Opposite Meanings — 37-38
5. Odd Ones Out — 38-39
6. Missing Word — 39-41
7. Mixed Examples — 41-42

Chapter One
ALPHABET REASONING
1. Letter Sequencing

There are six things to look for in **Letter Sequencing**:

a. Basic Sequences	1. Alphabetical Order 2. Forwards and Backwards Movement 3. Leapfrogging
b. Complex Sequences	4. Constant Gaps 5. Increasing or Decreasing Gaps 6. Alternating Gaps

An alphabet is always provided to help with the questions.

a. Basic Sequences

Basic Sequences have three main features:
1. All letter sequences follow **Alphabetical Order**.
2. The sequences can move **Forwards** and **Backwards**.
3. The sequences are established by **Leapfrogging** (jumping over one or more letters).

Example 1: Write the next letter in the sequence:
G P H Q I R ?

- This sequence is alphabetical like all other sequences.
- This sequence has a forwards movement.
- There is leapfrogging. It is necessary to jump over letters to establish the sequence.

G P H Q I R **J** (Answer)

Example 2: Write the next letter in the sequence:
Q X P Y O Z ?

Q X P Y O Z 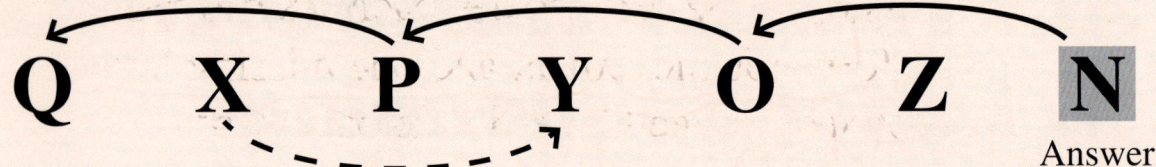 N

Answer

This is an alphabetical, leapfrogging sequence, but there is also a backwards and a forwards movement.

A B C D E F G H I J K L M N O P Q R S T U V W X Y Z

Exercise 1: 1a Write the two missing letters:
1) AD BE CF DG EH __FI__
2) CD EF GH IJ KL __MN__
3) KZ LY MX NW OV __PU__
4) DE ST FG UV HI __WX__
5) YR ZQ AP BO CN __DM__

b. Complex Sequences

4. There can be a **Constant Gap** (or same number of missing letters) between the letters in a sequence. Sequences can be solved either by writing in the missing letters or by counting the gaps between the letters.

Example: Write the next letter in the sequence:
C V E T G R ?

(Count 2 forwards C $\xrightarrow{+1}$ D $\xrightarrow{+1}$ E)

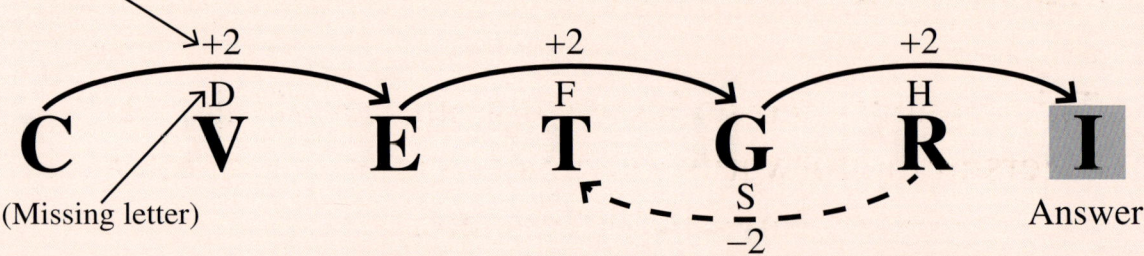

(Missing letter)   Answer

A plus sign (+) shows forwards movement and a minus sign (−) shows backwards movement.

There is one missing letter between each leapfrogged letter in the forwards movement and one missing letter between each leapfrogged letter in the backwards movement of the sequence.

A B C D E F G H I J K L M N O P Q R S T U V W X Y Z

Exercise 1: 1b   Write the two missing letters:

6) MW OU QS SQ UO   WM

7) JN KP LR MT NV   OX

8) DN FL HJ JH LF   ND

9) PA OY NW MU LS   KQ

10) OA RD UG XJ AM   DP

Record scores out of ten here
10

5. Sequences often have **Increasing** or **Decreasing** spaces between the letters.

Example: Write the next letter in the sequence:
D   E   G   J   N   ?

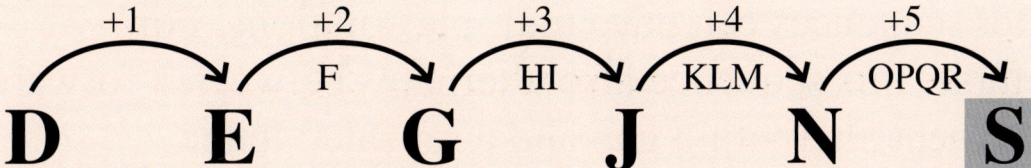

Answer

This sequence has an increasing number of missing letters in the forwards movement - no missing letters, 1 missing letter, 2 missing letters, etc.

A B C D E F G H I J K L M N O P Q R S T U V W X Y Z

Exercise 1: 2a Write the two missing letters:

1) KE KF LH NK QO __UT__
2) ZP UK QG ND LB __KA__
3) AB ZC XE UH QL __LQ__
4) UC VE XG AI EK __IM__
5) BC DD GF KI PM __UR__ ✗ VR

6. Sequences often have **Alternating Gaps** between the letters.

Example: Write the next letter in the sequence:
L N N Q Q S S V ?

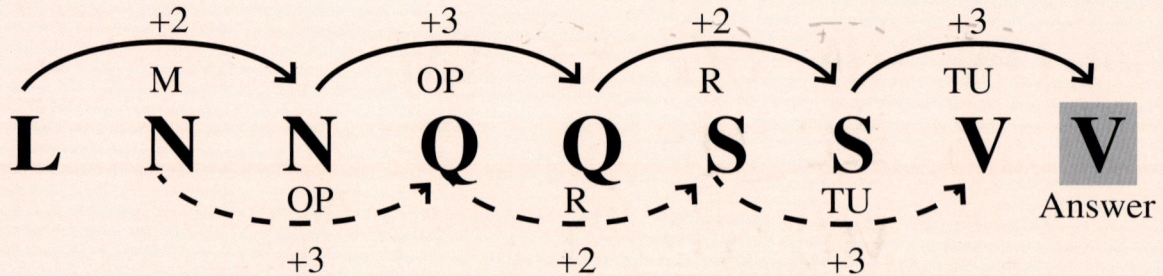

This sequence alternates between 1 missing letter and 2 missing letters in a forwards leapfrogging movement.

Letter sequences can have multiple solutions. For example, this sequence also alternates between a forwards movement alternating gap and a repeated letter.

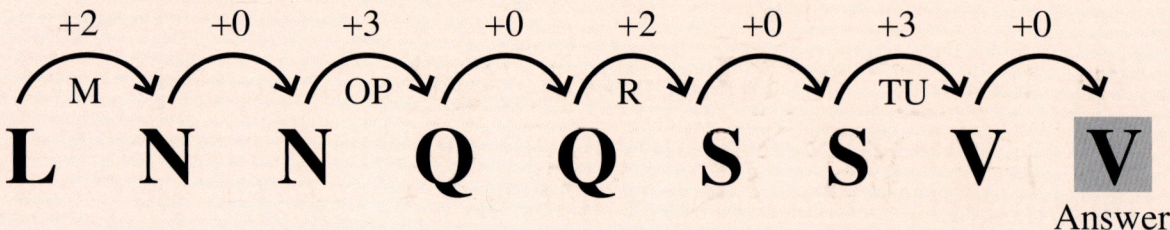

A B C D E F G H I J K L M N O P Q R S T U V W X Y Z

Exercise 1: 2b   Write the two missing letters:

6) AB CD DF FH GJ __IL__

7) NP MO JL IK FH __EG__

8) SJ VI YG BF ED __MC__

9) GR GT HV HX IZ __IB__

10) HI JK KL MN NO __PQ__

Score: 9

c. Mixed Examples

Exercise 1: 3   Write the two missing letters:

1) MZ OX QV ST UR __WP__

2) AB YZ CD WX EF __UV__

3) RA RC QE QG PI __PK__

4) LP MO OM RJ VF __AA__

5) DU GS JQ MO PM __SK__

6) KR MT NU PW QX __SZ__

7) WK TJ SI PH OG __LF__

8) CS DT EU FV GW __HX__

9) EF HI KL NO QR __IU__

10) PQ RS TU VW XY __ZA__

Score: 10

23/09

STOP

© 2012 Stephen Curran

2. Alphabet Codes

An alphabet is always provided to help with the questions. There are two basic categories of **Alphabet Codes**:

a. Plus and Minus Codes   a) Letter to Letter Code
  b) Word to Code
  c) Code to Word

b. Position Codes (by counting position in the alphabet)

a. Plus and Minus Codes

a) **Letter to Letter Code**

This is the simplest type of **Plus and Minus Code**. A Letter to Letter relationship is established with either a forwards or backwards movement in the alphabet.

Example: Write the missing letters:
HC is to **KX** as **YP** is to **?**

1. The alphabet is given and gaps between the letters are counted forwards and backwards to give the code.

   − ← A B C D E F G H I J K L M N O P Q R S T U V W X Y Z → +

   − The next backwards letter would be **Z**.
   The next forwards letter would be **A**. +

2. Movement 1 (**H** to **K**) is a forwards movement of **Plus 3** on the alphabet (count the gaps and not the letters).

3. Movement 2 (**C** to **X**) is a backwards movement of **Minus 5** on the alphabet.

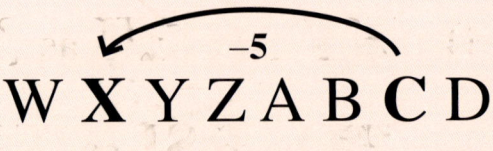

4. This movement can be shown on the following grid: $\dfrac{+3\ |\ -5}{H\ |\ C}$ is to **KX**

5. Movements 1 and 2 are now applied to the letters **YP**. $\dfrac{+3\ |\ -5}{Y\ |\ P}$ is to **?**

6. Apply the forwards movement of **Plus 3** to the letter **Y**.

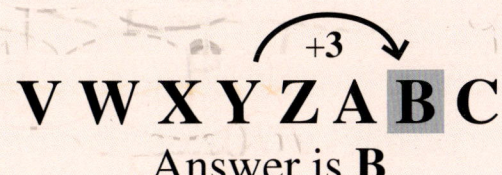
V W X Y Z A **B** C
Answer is **B**

7. Apply the backwards movement of **Minus 5** to the letter **P**.

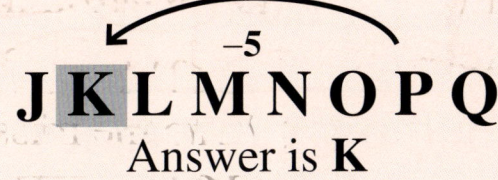
J **K** L M N O P Q
Answer is **K**

The answer is: **BK**

A B C D E F G H I J K L M N O P Q R S T U V W X Y Z

Exercise 1: 4a   Write the missing letters:

Score

1) **DE** is to **HI** as **RS** is to **?** ⟶ VW

2) **IR** is to **LW** as **DT** is to **?** ⟶ GY

3) **AO** is to **YM** as **CQ** is to **?** ⟶ AO

4) **XY** is to **RU** as **JK** is to **?** ⟶ DG

5) **PL** is to **SI** as **NH** is to **?** ⟶ QE

b) Word to Code

This is the second type of Plus and Minus Code. A Word to Code relationship is established again with either a forwards or backwards movement in the alphabet. The same rules apply except that words are used, which permit longer and more complex codes.

> Example: If the code for **CAT** is **FCW**, what is the code for **DOG**?

1. Work out the code by counting the gaps forwards or backwards on the alphabet. This word to code relationship only counts forwards.

   Backwards ← −   **Forwards** + →

   A B C D E F G H I J K L M N O P Q R S T U V W X Y Z
      +3 ↗ and so on

2. The movement can be shown on the following grid:

+3	+2	+3
C	A	T

   will give: **FCW**

3. The grid and alphabet can now be used to create the new code.

   Backwards ← −   **Forwards** + →

   A B C D E F G H I J K L M N O P Q R S T U V W X Y Z
      +3 ↗ and so on

+3	+2	+3
D	O	G

   will give the answer: **GQJ**

A B C D E F G H I J K L M N O P Q R S T U V W X Y Z

Exercise 1: 4b Write the missing code:

6) If the code for **BACK** is **DCEM**,
   what is the code for **THEM**? _____VJGO_____

7) If the code for **STONE** is **TVRRJ**,
   what is the code for **ROCKS**? _____SQFOT_____

8) If the code for **BLINK** is **ZJGLI**,
   what is the code for **WINKS**? _____UGLJO_____

9) If the code for **TRACK** is **SPXYF**,
   what is the code for **RAILS**? _____QYFHN_____

10) If the code for **PROVE** is **PTOXE**,
    what is the code for **ALLOW**? _____ANLQW_____

c) Code to Word

This is the third type of Plus and Minus Code. This time a Code to Word relationship is established with either a forwards or backwards movement in the alphabet.

There is one major difference; all Code to Word types require a **reversal of the original forwards or backwards movement** to create the word.

Example: If the code for **RUN** is **OSM**, what does **GMF** stand for?

1. Work out the code on the alphabet as before by counting forwards or backwards. This code counts backwards.

Backwards — ⟵
Forwards + ⟶

A B C D E F G H I J K L M N O P Q R S T U V W X Y Z

−3 and so on

2. The movement can be shown on the following grid:

OSM ⟵

−3	−2	−1
R	U	N

3. The grid and alphabet can now be used to create the new word. It must be **reversed** because we have to go back to a word from a code.

Backwards — ⟵
Forwards + ⟶

A B C D E F G H I J K L M N O P Q R S T U V W X Y Z

+3 and so on

+3	+2	+1
G	M	F

⟶ **JOG**
Answer

A B C D E F G H I J K L M N O P Q R S T U V W X Y Z

Exercise 1: 5a   Write the missing letters:

1) If the code for **DOG** is **FQI**, what does **NCR** stand for?   _pet LAP_

A B C D E F G H I J K L M N O P Q R S T U V W X Y Z

2) If the code for **MAY** is **JXV**, what does **IBQ** stand for? ~~FYN~~ LET

3) If the code for **NOT** is **OQW**, what does **XCJ** stand for? ~~YEM~~ WAG

4) If the code for **CAR** is **CBT**, what does **VBP** stand for? ~~VCR~~ VAN

5) If the code for **TEA** is **SCX**, what does **BSM** stand for? ~~AQJ~~ CUP

b. Position (Mirror) Codes STOP

Checked SW 30/9

Position or **Mirror Codes** can easily be confused with Plus and Minus Codes as the questions are set out in an identical way.

Example: If the code for **HEM** is **SVN**, what is the code for **TOY**?

a. Position or Mirror Codes are created by reflecting a word or code from one half of the alphabet to the other.

b. The alphabet has 26 letters. If it is divided into two halves there will be 13 letters on each side.

13 letters from A to M   13 letters from N to Z
A B C D E F G H I J K L M | N O P Q R S T U V W X Y Z

© 2012 Stephen Curran

1. **HEM** is created by counting from the nearest point to either end of the first half of the alphabet. **H** count left 6; **E** count right 5; **M** count left 1 letter(s).

2. **SVN** is a mirror reflection on the other side of the alphabet. **S** count right 6; **V** count left 5; **N** count right 1 letter(s).

3. If we now view the whole alphabet we can see the reflection, or mirror effect, of the word and the code.

To find the new code we repeat the same mirroring process.

4. **TOY** is created in the same way as above. **T** count right 7; **O** count right 2; **Y** count left 2 letters.

5. Now we can create the missing code. **G** count left 7; **L** count left 2; **B** count right 2 letters.

6. The word **TOY** is reflected to make the code **GLB**.

The answer is: GLB

A B C D E F G H I J K L M N O P Q R S T U V W X Y Z

Exercise 1: 5b Write the missing letters:

6) If the code for **LAMP** is **OZNK**, what is the code for **BULB**? _YFOY_

7) If the code for **WASP** is **DZHK**, what is the code for **BEES**? _FYVVH_

8) If **WANTS** is written in code as **DZMGH**, what is the code for **NEEDS**? _MVVWH_

9) If the code for **PLAY** is **KOZB**, what is the code for **WORK**? _DLIPS_

10) If **BOAT** is written in code as **YLZG**, what is the code for **FISH**? _URHS_

Score

c. Mixed Examples

A B C D E F G H I J K L M N O P Q R S T U V W X Y Z

Exercise 1: 6 Write the missing letters:

Score

1) a) **BD** is to **DF** as **RV** is to ? _TX_

   b) **NO** is to **KL** as **UV** is to ? _RS_

2) a) **AE** is to **FJ** as **KO** is to ? _PT_

   b) **VZ** is to **QU** as **YC** is to ? _TX_

A B C D E F G H I J K L M N O P Q R S T U V W X Y Z

3) a) **FG** is to **HE** as **OP** is to **?** __QN__

   b) **DE** is to **BH** as **TU** is to **?** __RS__ ✗ __RX__

4) a) **AB** is to **FW** as **DE** is to **?** __IZ__

   b) **WX** is to **YV** as **QR** is to **?** __SP__

5) a) **RS** is to **VW** as **IS** is to **?** __MW__

   b) **PQ** is to **TM** as **NO** is to **?** __RS__ ✗ __RK__

6) If the code for **WRONG** is **UPMLE**, what is the code for **RIGHT**? __PGEFR__

7) If the code for **HORSE** is **SLIHV**, what is the code for **PONIES**? __KLMRVH__

8) If **LETTER** in code is **MGWXJX**, what is the code for **BOOKS**? __CQROX__

9) If the code for **FILMS** is **EGIIN**, what is the code for **PLAYS**? __OJXUN__

10) If the code for **DRUMS** is **WJFNH**, what is the code for **PIANO**? __KRZML__

Chapter Two
WORD PATTERNS and CODES
1. Word Patterns

Word Pattern questions involve the use of numbering to discover one new word from a given word or words. There are two types of question:

a. Finding a missing word from a **One Word Pattern**.
b. Finding a missing word from a **Two Word Pattern**.

a. One Word Pattern

In **One Word Pattern** questions, two pairs of words are given. The missing word is found by applying the number pattern that links the word pairs.

Example:
> Find the missing word:
> (relied deer) (larger real)
> (mallet ?)

1. Number the first word. The letters are now represented by numbers. Number the second word accordingly.

$$\begin{matrix} & & & & & & & 5\,2 \\ 1\,2\,3\,4\,5\,6 & & & 6\,2\,5\,1 \end{matrix}$$
relied deer

2. Number the second pair of words to clarify which letters should be chosen to make the correct pattern.

$$1\,2\,3\,4\,5\,6 \quad 6\,5\,2\,1$$
larger real

© 2012 Stephen Curran

3. Number the word in the third grouping and repeat the number pattern to find the missing word.

1 2 34 5 6   6 5 2 1
mallet   **?**

4. Now create the new word by using the pattern.

6 5 2 1
Answer: **team**

Exercise 2: 1   Fill in the missing word:

Score

1) (**pace**   **ape**)   (**race**   **are**)
        (**rice**   **?**)   ire

2) (**gram**   **ram**)   (**grim**   **rim**)
        (**plot**   **?**)   lot

3) (**glide**   **lid**)   (**blade**   **lad**)
        (**sled**   **?**)   led

4) (**crazy**   **cry**)   (**trendy**   **try**)
        (**pound**   **?**)   pod

5) (**wants**   **swan**)   (**roped**   **drop**)
        (**hopes**   **?**)   shop

6) (**chimp**   **chip**)   (**short**   **shot**)
        (**clout**   **?**)   clot

7) (blonde   bone)   (pounds   puns)
      (fringe   ?) _fire_

8) (barrier   rear)   (rampart   trap)
      (toenail   ?) _lion_

9) (streams   seat)   (bureaux   beau)
      (dewater   ?) _date_

10) (drill   lid)   (trade   eat)
      (beast   ?) _tab_

b. Two Word Pattern

In **Two Word Pattern** questions, two sets of words are given. The middle word of the first set has been made from the outer two words. The middle word of the second set must be found.

Example: Find the missing word:
(garage [goat] lottery)   (sorrow [?] staple)

1. Number the middle word of the first set of words in numerical order.

$$\overset{1\ 2\ 3\ 4}{\textbf{(garage [goat] lottery)}}$$

2. Using the numbers from the middle word, number each of the common letters from the two words either side.

$$\overset{1\ 3\quad 3\ 1\quad\ 1\ 2\ 3\ 4\quad 2\ 4\ 4}{\textbf{(garage [goat] lottery)}}$$

3. Number the second set of outer words in the same way.

$$\overset{1\ 3\quad 3\ 1}{(\textbf{sorrow}} \ [\ \overset{1\ 2\ 3\ 4}{\ \ \ \ }\ ] \ \overset{2\ 4\ 4}{\textbf{staple})}$$

4. Number the missing space and write the various alternatives from the outer words below it.

$$\overset{1\ 3\quad 3\ 1}{(\textbf{sorrow}} \ [\ \overset{1\ 2\ 3\ 4}{\underset{\underset{o\ \ \ \ r\ \ \ p}{s\ \ t\ \ o\ \ a}}{\ \ \ \ }}\ ] \ \overset{2\ 4\ 4}{\textbf{staple})}$$

5. Write in the letters where there are no choices.

$$\overset{1\ 2\ 3\ 4}{[\underset{\underset{o\ \ \ \ r\ \ \ p}{s\ \ t\ \ o\ \ a}}{\textbf{t}}]}$$

6. Select the correct letters to create the missing word. There is only ever one correct answer.

Answer: **[s t o p]**

Exercise 2: 2 Fill in the missing word:  Score: 10

1) (s**à**nd [**fàde**] f**ǎce**)   (s**ȯ**f**a** [soar] s**o**u**r**)
   $\overset{2\ \ 3}{}\ \overset{1234}{}\ \overset{1234}{}$ $\overset{\ \ 2\ 3}{}\ \overset{1234}{}\ \overset{12\ \ 4}{}$

2) (st**ew** [**flew**] l**eaf**)   (f**eta** [tova] **over**)
   $\overset{34}{}\ \overset{1234}{}\ \overset{2\ 3\ 1}{}$ $\overset{1234}{}$

3) (heat [boat] above)   (rate [late] plait)

4) (left [gift] right)   (book [cook] socks)

5) (first [star] faces)   (cargo [tour] guilt)

6) (fried [fold] mould)   (twice [tape] taupe)

7) (cater [ate] apple)   (drink [rig] cling)

8) (letter [reed] pound)   (jacket [tear] diner)

9) (pencil [prune] ruler)   (candy [crane] raved)

10) (nearby [born] factory)   (kettle [link] ceiling)

2. Secret Code

In **Secret Code** questions some codes and words are given. The codes are not written in the same order as the words and one word or code can be irrelevant to the question.

Example: Find the correct code for each word.
BAR   TAN   ARC   CAT
568   456   857

As a starting point look for:
Letter(s) in the same position in two or more words.
Letter(s) at the opposing ends of two or more words.

1. Letter **A** is in the same position in **BAR**, **TAN** and **CAT**.
   Letter **T** begins **TAN** and ends **CAT**.
   Letter **C** begins **CAT** and ends **ARC**.

2. **BAR** and **ARC** are linked together as **AR** are in the same order in both words. **AR** must be **56** as these numbers occur twice in the codes.

	4 5 6	5 6 8
Answer:	BAR	ARC

3. **CAT** and **TAN** are linked together because they both have the letters **A** and **T**. **TAN** cannot be the correct word because there is no code number for **N**.

4. We know from **ARC** that **C** is **8**. Therefore **CAT** must be **857**.

	8 5 7
Answer:	CAT

Exercise 2: 3 Find the answers to the following:

START	CHART	STARS	PARTS
1234	57342	1234१	63421
63421	12341	57342	12342

1) Find the code for the word **PATCH**. 63257
2) Find the code for the word **TRAPS**. 24361
3) Find the code for the word **CHAPS**. 57361
4) Which word has the code **53421**? CARTS
5) Which word has the code **53257**? CATCH

PROVE	GROOVE	GROVE	GRAVE
62357	123357	12357	12457
12457	62357	123357	12357

6) Find the code for the word **VERGE**. 57217

7) Find the code for the word **RAVER**. 24572
8) Find the code for the word **GRAPE**. 12467
9) Which word has the code **6772**? PEER
10) Which word has the code **41277**? AGREE

Score: 10

3. Mixed Examples

Exercise 2: 4 Answer the following: Score: 10

1) (**garner** ¹²³⁴⁵⁶ **earn** ⁵²³⁴) (**hoarse** ¹²³⁴⁵⁶ **soar** ⁵²³⁴)
   (**master** ¹²³⁴⁵⁶ ?) ⁵²³⁴ east

2) (**mantras** ¹²³⁴⁵⁶⁷ **tram** ⁴⁵²¹) (**depress** ¹²³⁴⁵⁶⁷ **reed** ⁴⁵²¹)
   (**lantern** ¹²³⁴⁵⁶⁷ ?) ⁴⁵²¹ teal

3) (**boomed** ¹²³⁴⁵⁶ **mood** ⁴³²⁶) (**flambé** ¹²³⁴⁵⁶ **male** ⁴³²⁶)
   (**plague** ¹²³⁴⁵⁶ ?) ⁴³²⁶ gale

4) (**winch** ³¹² [**chip**] ¹²³⁴ **snips**) (**least** ³¹³ [**STEP**] ¹²³⁴ **drape**)

5) (**barge** ⁴³² [**crab**] ¹ **coach** ³) (**balls** ⁴³² [**SLAB**] ¹ **spire**)

6) (**storm** ³⁴ [**must**] ¹ **sound** ²) (**steam** ³⁴ [**MAST**] ¹ **bland** ²)

SPOON	SCONES	CONES	CLOSE
14332	57316	153261	53261
14332	153261	53261	525316

7) Find the code for the word **LOOSE**. 73316
8) Find the code for the word **COLON**. 53732
9) Which word has the code **57326**? CLONE
10) Which word has the code **17346**? SLOPE

8₂ 21/10.

Chapter Three
VOCABULARY with SPELLING

> These techniques require basic spelling skills and the ability to recognise words (but not necessarily their meaning).

1. Letter Shift

In **Letter Shift** questions one letter is moved from the first word to the second word, to make two new words. No other rearrangement takes place and the new words make sense.

Example: Move one letter from the first word to the second word to make two new words from:
CRAVE and **COW**

1. Try removing each letter at a time from the first word to see what new words can be made:

CRAVE The **C** can be removed to make **RAVE**.
The **R** can be removed to make **CAVE**.

2. Test which letter can be placed in the second word by spreading out the letters so there is space to try out the possibilities. The **C** will not fit into the word anywhere, but the **R** will fit into the second word.

C̸RAVE and CᴿO W

3. Write out the two new words:
CAVE and **CROW**

Exercise 3: 1   Answer the following:

1) **GLADE** and **MAN**   become   Glad   and   Mane
2) **PLANT** and **RAP**   become   plan   and   trap
3) **GLOAT** and **COVE**   become   _____ and _____
4) **GRAVE** and **CHAT**   become   _____ and _____
5) **CREATE** and **BARD**   become   _____ and _____
6) **LEAPT** and **ABLE**   become   _____ and _____
7) **ROVES** and **NETS**   become   _____ and _____
8) **TREND** and **LEAN**   become   _____ and _____
9) **PRAISED** and **LAID**   become   _____ and _____
10) **PLAYER** and **RISE**   become   _____ and _____

2. Compound Word

In **Compound Word** questions it is necessary to find two words, one from each group, that together make one correctly spelt word without changing the order of the letters. The word from the first group always comes first.

Example: Combine two words to make a compound word.   **(at head long)**
(ring rest home)

If a quick scan of the words does not give the answer, try writing out the nine possibilities. The two words placed together will often trigger the correct answer.

© 2012 Stephen Curran

atring atrest athome headring **headrest**
headhome longring longrest longhome

'headring' looks like a word but it is not in the dictionary. None of the other combinations gives recognisable words. The only real possibility is **'headrest'** and this is a word.

The answer is: **head rest** (the word is **headrest**).

Exercise 3: 2   Write the compound word:

Score

1) **(good life hand)**
   (time thing death)
   Lifetime

2) **(flat ham hand)**
   (mock pack land)
   _____

3) **(real too any)**
   (body large other)
   _____

4) **(butter flat gain)**
   (cap time cup)
   buttercup

5) **(gold pram mast)**
   (fish gain chip)
   _____

6) **(heel leg foot)**
   (long print toe)
   _____

7) **(grace black boast)**
   (bored board full)
   _____

8) **(bad rail car)**
   (road train horn)
   _____

9) **(cape fast ring)**
   (let pull stop)
   _____

10) **(care wind much)**
    (less ring pets)
    _____

Many compound words are **elisions** of two words. This means there is a change of sound when the words merge.

Example: Combine two words to make a compound word. **(gad toe rib)** **(gone get tell)**

The answer is: **gad get** (the word is **gadget**). As separate words, **gad** and **get** sound different from when they are merged together as **gadget**. The **d** and **g** make a **j** sound when elided.

Exercise 3: 3   Write the compound word:

Score

1) (met poor mind)
   (able lay hod)
   method

2) (prime pan pant)
   (time try lent)
   _____

3) (grow link bored)
   (less age robe)
   _____

4) (inner orb enter)
   (it note room)
   _____

5) (back waist clip)
   (coat card pain)
   _____

6) (plan band poor)
   (net age lay)
   bandage

7) (grim flat meat)
   (fish wall ace)
   _____

8) (stay hand hear)
   (some ache wear)
   _____

9) (high know pact)
   (wire chin ledge)
   _____

10) (rat miss hair)
    (age trip her)
    _____

3. Hidden Word

In these sentences, a **Hidden Word** of four letters must be found at the end of one word and the beginning of the next word.

Example: Find the hidden four-letter word in the sentence:
Nobody should look after your gear.

1. Scan the line looking carefully at the beginning and end of words to see if you can spot the word immediately.

2. If this does not work, use the following technique:

Using your thumbs, cover four letters at the beginning and end of words. When working across two words there are three possibilities. **In multiple-choice papers this technique can be applied directly on the answer sheet.** In this example, these two words hold the answer.

3 - 1	2 - 2	1 - 3
y**our g**ear	yo**ur ge**ar	you**r gea**r
ourg is not a word.	urge is a word.	rgea is not a word.

The answer is: **urge** (yo**ur ge**ar)

Exercise 3: 4   Write the four-letter word:

(The questions are printed larger to enable you to practise your technique.)

Score

1) There was no way out of the burning building. _____

2) The chimp lay down on the straw. _____

3) The children tried to climb the tree. _____

4) He was praised for his efforts. _____

5) It was very scenic rowing down the river. _____

6) The film star was rich and famous. _____

7) He bought an ice cream from the shop. _____

8) The climb up the hill was very arduous. _____

9) Having rambled for hours the walkers were extremely tired. _____

10) The assault course was our biggest challenge. _____

4. Missing Letter

In **Missing Letter** questions, the same letter must fit into both sets of brackets to complete the word in front of the brackets and begin the word after the brackets.

Example: Find the missing letter that completes all four words.

ree [?] oan
fow [?] obe

1. Go through the alphabet. Is it **a**? Is it **b**? etc. and try out these letters in the spaces in a standard test.

2. **Note that multiple-choice tests give five alternatives, so these can be immediately tried out in the spaces.**

The missing letter is **l**:

ree [l] oan
fow [l] obe

The four words are: **reel loan fowl lobe**

Exercise 3: 5   Fill in the missing letter:

Score

1) **chi [?] ort**
   cha [?] int
   The letter is ____ .

2) **las [?] rip**
   par [?] own
   The letter is ____ .

3) **grai [?] ail**
   plai [?] est
   The letter is ____ .

4) **sno [?] orn**
   gro [?] aist
   The letter is ____ .

5) **pla [?] awn**
   awa [?] acht
   The letter is ____ .

6) **blac [?] nife**
   por [?] neel
   The letter is ____ .

7) **brin [?] lade**
   kin [?] naw
   The letter is ____ .

8) **chin [?] corn**
   who [?] gain
   The letter is ____ .

9) **gra [?] ast**
   plu [?] ite
   The letter is ____ .

10) **cub [?] asy**
    din [?] ast
    The letter is ____ .

5. Mixed Examples

Exercise 3: 6

Move one letter to make two new words:

1) **FRONT** and **AMP**   become   _____ and _____

2) **CHIMP** and **ALL**   become   _____ and _____

Join two words to make a compound word:

3) (**star   tars   slip**)
   (**trip   chin   light**)
   _____

4) (**stop   nest   book**)
   (**bird   let   dogs**)
   _____

5) (**book   motor   hill**)
   (**way   less   all**)
   _____

Find the hidden four-letter word in the sentence:

6) Their mountain climb was slow and difficult.
   _____

7) It was cold and snowy last winter. _____

Find the missing letter that completes all four words:

8) **firs [?] ram**
   las [?] rack
   The letter is ___ .

9) **eas [?] arl**
   pleas [?] ast
   The letter is ___ .

10) **cra [?] ack**
    cri [?] lack
    The letter is ___ .

Score

Chapter Four
VOCABULARY with MEANING

These techniques require an ability to recognise words and understand their meaning within the context of a sentence. Good spelling skills help this recognition process, but many children can read and understand words they cannot spell.

1. Analogy

An **Analogy** is a similarity in meaning between two parallel statements or words. This comparison is linked by the word 'as' which means 'like'.

Example: | Write the word that will complete the analogy. | **Cheer** is to catcall as **applaud** is to (show   boo   clap) |

1. Read the possibilities carefully and try and identify the basis of comparison. Here the basis of similarity between the two statements is signs of audience response.

2. Having decided the basis of comparison, try each option to find the analogy that works best.

The correct answer is boo. It should read:
Cheer is to **catcall** as **applaud** is to **boo**

Exercise 4: 1

Write the word that will complete the analogy:

Score

1) **Up** is to **down** as **dim** is to (wrong left bright)
_____

2) **Ear** is to **hear** as **eye** is to (sight see look)
_____

3) **Love** is to **hate** as **laugh** is to (try cry giggle)
_____

4) **Boat** is to **sail** as **plane** is to (fly flight sky)
_____

5) **Summer** is to **hot** as **winter** is to (cold snow rain)
_____

6) **Four** is to **eight** as **six** is to (three twelve sixteen)
_____

7) **Cat** is to **kitten** as **dog** is to (bark puppy walk)
_____

8) **Part** is to **trap** as **snip** is to (snap port pins)
_____

9) **Finger** is to **hand** as **toe** is to (foot boot shoe)
_____

10) **Bring** is to brought as **fight** is to (fright fought court)
_____

© 2012 Stephen Curran

2. Similar Meanings (Synonyms)

In these questions it is necessary to find two words, one from each group, that are most **Similar in Meaning**.

Example: Which two words are similar in meaning?
(peaceful   war   destroy)
(pain   love   feud)

1. Scan both sets of words to see if you can spot the answer immediately. If this does not work move on to step 2.

2. Compare each of the nine possibilities:

   peaceful - pain; peaceful - love; peaceful - feud
   war - pain; war - love; **war - feud**
   destroy - pain; destroy - love; destroy - feud

3. Test the words in a sentence: 'A **war** broke out' and 'A **feud** broke out'. They should be the same part of speech and convey the same meaning.

The correct answer is: **war - feud**

Exercise 4: 2   Write the two words closest in meaning: Score

1) (sand   bucket   flag)
   (pail   spade   bag)
   _____ _____

2) (bread   slice   cheese)
   (pickle   roll   butter)
   _____ _____

3) (stalk   root   leaf)
   (stem   follow   tall)
   _____ _____

4) (jump   run   stamp)
   (walk   hop   stroll)
   _____ _____

5) (neck   shoulder   brow)
   (nose   cheek   throat)
   _____ _____

6) (break   brake   drop)
   (fix   smash   rise)
   _____ _____

7) (woman toddler man)   8) (toddle fly run)
   (lady girl child)   (race jog swim)
   _____ _____   _____ _____

9) (play sleep other)   10) (grip catch slap)
   (rest wake round)   (slip clutch caught)
   _____ _____   _____ _____

3. Word Link (Homonyms)

In **Word Link** questions two pairs of words are given. A choice of five words is given in the answers. Only one of these words will go equally well with both of these pairs.

Example: Which word below will link the two pairs of bracketed words?

(injure   offend)
(coiled   looped)

hurt, smash, straight, wound, twist

1. Scan the answers to see if the word link is obvious.
2. If it is not, think of alternative meanings as these words are homonyms and have more than one meaning.
3. Invent sentences and substitute the words, e.g. 'I can hurt someone' works with the first pair: 'I can **injure**' and 'I can **offend**' but no sentence using 'hurt' will work with **looped** and **coiled**.
4. Continue this process until the word link is found, e.g. 'I can **injure**' or 'I can **offend**' works with 'I can **wound**'. Also, 'A rope can be **wound**.' It can also be 'coiled' or 'looped.'

The word link for both pairs is: **wound**

Exercise 4: 3 Write the word link for the word pairs:

1) (method   way)
   (law   order)

   Possible word links:

   road, rule, type,
   legal, boss

   _____

2) (insult   snub)
   (slim   slender)

   Possible word links:

   grip, slight, thin,
   ignore, send

   _____

3) (leave   depart)
   (energy   drive)

   Possible word links:

   come, car, go,
   exit, verve

   _____

4) (kit   apparatus)
   (confront   stop)

   Possible word links:

   give, tackle, tools,
   halt, bend

   _____

5) (subtract   minus)
   (steal   swipe)

   Possible word links:

   minor, let, take,
   steel, hit

   _____

6) (piece   portion)
   (fraction   area)

   Possible word links:

   divide, slip, section,
   part, zone

   _____

7) (cash   coins)
   (switch   trade)

   Possible word links:

   money, sell, change,
   buy, purchase

   _____

8) (level   smooth)
   (maisonette   apartment)

   Possible word links:

   low, flat, even,
   house, caravan

   _____

9) (vessel   boat)
   (art   skill)

   Possible word links:

   craft, ship, paint,
   cup, talent

   _____

10) (lotion   ointment)
    (elite   prime)

    Possible word links:

    first, salve, sole,
    cream, best

    _____

Score

4. Opposite Meanings (Antonyms)

In these questions it is necessary to find two words, one from each group, that are most **Opposite in Meaning**.

Example: Which two words, one from each bracketed group, are most opposite in meaning?

(agree   curse   denial)
(swear   belief   blessing)

1. Scan both sets of words to see if you can spot the answer immediately. If this does not work move on to step 2.

2. Carefully compare each of the nine possibilities. The answer must be the most opposite in meaning:

   agree - swear;   agree - belief;   agree - blessing
   curse - swear;   curse - belief;   **curse - blessing**
   denial - swear;   denial - belief;   denial - blessing

3. Test out the words in a sentence. They should be the same part of speech and give the opposite meaning, e.g. 'A person can utter a **blessing**', 'A person can utter a **curse**'.

   The correct answer is: **curse - blessing**

Exercise 4: 4 Write the words most opposite in meaning:

Score

1) (front up side)
   (font back left)
   _____ _____

2) (cheap laze sweet)
   (tweet expensive box)
   _____ _____

3) (undo try trick)
   (bind double thread)
   _____ _____

4) (climb decent play)
   (jump slip descend)
   _____ _____

5) (rich greedy large)
   (wealthy poor tasty)
   _____ _____

6) (break take brake)
   (pattern make leave)
   _____ _____

7) (conceal control contrast)
   (reveal prove change)
   _____ _____

8) (taken gift take)
   (gave give grave)
   _____ _____

9) (happy hoping place)
   (pleased miserable meal)
   _____ _____

10) (rage range engaged)
    (engrossed calm slip)
    _____ _____

5. Odd Ones Out

In these questions, three of the five words are related in some way. Two words are not related to the other three; they are **Odd Ones Out** and must be identified.

Example: Which two words are the odd ones out?

**veal   legumes   mutton
tubers   venison**

1. **Veal**, **mutton** and **venison** can be linked as they are kinds of meat.
2. **Legumes** (seeds and pods) and **tubers** (roots) are both types of vegetables.

The odd ones out are: **legumes** and **tubers**

Exercise 4: 5   Write the odd ones out:

1) fast, slow, speedy, quick, sedate

2) star, planet, alien, spirit, moon

3) climb, raise, lower, ascend, descend

4) frog, newt, bear, cow, dog

5) shout, whisper, croak, holler, scream

6) biscuit, crisps, cola, water, cake

7) pencil, pen, ruler, rubber, crayon

8) place, point, gold, position, silver

9) envelope, stamp, stomp, letter, packet

10) type, write, sort, kind, wrote

Score

6. Missing Word

In these questions, the word in capitals has had three consecutive letters removed. These three letters will make one correctly spelt **Missing Word** without changing their order.

© 2012 Stephen Curran

Example: What is the missing three-letter word?

The scholar acquired great **LNING**.

Five possibilities are given in the answers section:

ARE   IRE   URN   EAR   ORE

1. Read the sentence carefully and think of the context. This may identify the three-letter word immediately. If this does not work move on to step 2:

2. Space out the letters. Try out the possibilities.

   EAR
   L   NING
   (LEARNING)

The correct three-letter word is: **EAR**

Exercise 4: 6   What is the missing three-letter word?

1) The magician made the rabbit **DISAPR**.
   The five possibilities are:
   PER PIE PEA EAR PEN   _____

2) The tourists saw disappointing **WS**.
   The five possibilities are:
   ARE VIE SET LIE CAR   _____

3) The ball went **THER** than expected.
   The five possibilities are:
   RAT SUN RAN FUR LAT   _____

4) He **ATDED** training every Monday and Thursday.
   The five possibilities are:
   HEN MEN TEN LEN LAN   _____

5) Do not despair - **TE** is still hope!
   The five possibilities are:
   ARE HEE HER MEN LAD   _____

6) The children were looking forward to their **HOAY**.
   The five possibilities are:
   LAD LID DAD DIN NOD   _____

7) The cats that we have as pets are **DOMESTIED**.
   The five possibilities are:
   DOG PET PAT CAN CAT   _____

8) The explorers were **PING** the coastline.
   The five possibilities are:
   MOP CAP CAT COP MAP   _____

9) The robins were **NESG** in the tree.
   The five possibilities are:
   TAN SIN BIN TIN TON   _____

10) The car was **FOLING** the signs for Thorpe Park.
    The five possibilities are:
    LOW BOW LAW SAW PIN   _____

Score

7. Mixed Examples

Exercise 4: 7   Answer the following:

Write the two words that are odd ones out.

1) car, bicycle, house, caravan, bus

2) dog, lion, hamster, gorilla, elephant

_____ _____   _____ _____

Write the word that will complete the analogy:

3) **Win** is to **lose**
   as **succeed** is to
   (chose   fail   rail)
   _____

4) **More** is to **less**
   as **misery** is to
   (sadness   joy   amuse)
   _____

Write the two words most similar in meaning:

5) (mate   enemy   foe)
   (meat   friend   meet)
   _____   _____

Write the two words most opposite in meaning:

6) (select   praise   need)
   (choose   repel   reject)
   _____   _____

Write the missing three-letter word:

7) The gardener **CPED** the hedge with shears.
   The five possibilities are:
   POP RIP LOT LIP ROB   _____

8) He watched the sheep **SHING** competition.
   The five possibilities are:
   EEL EAR ARE APE TEN   _____

Write the word link for the pairs of words:

9) (lose colour   bleach)
   (dim   lessen)

   Possible word links:
   faze, praise, darken,
   flue, fade
   _____

10) (vanish   decline)
    (diminish   die away)

    Possible word links:
    demean, dwindle,
    swindle, leave, lo
    _____

Score

PROGRESS CHARTS

Shade in your score for each exercise on the graph. Add up for your total score. An adult will work out the percentage.

1. ALPHABET REASONING

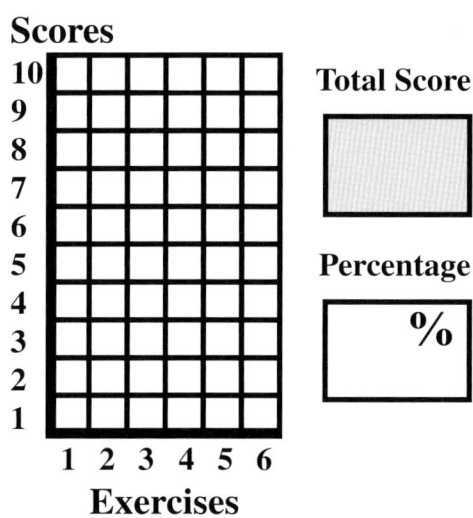

2. WORD PATTERNS AND CODES

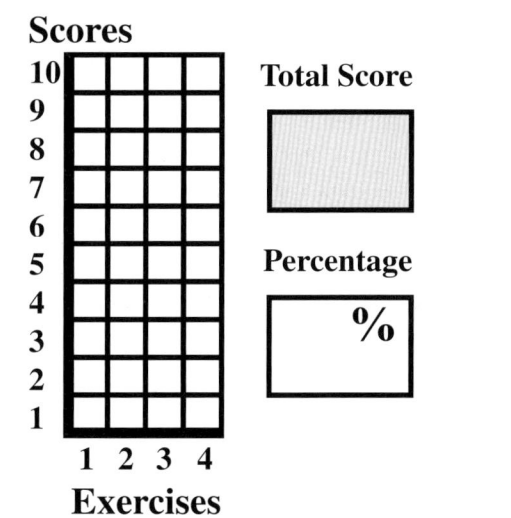

3. VOCABULARY WITH SPELLING

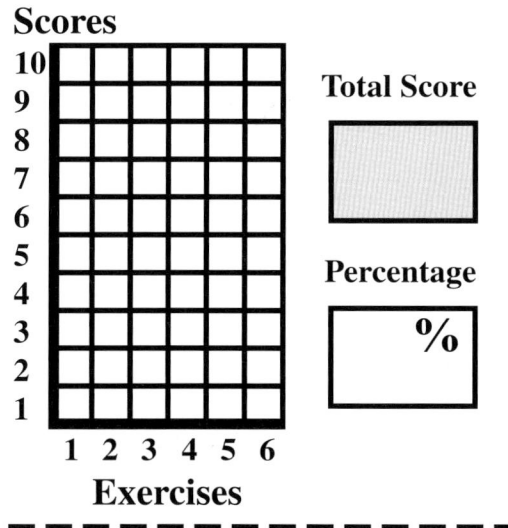

4. VOCABULARY WITH MEANING

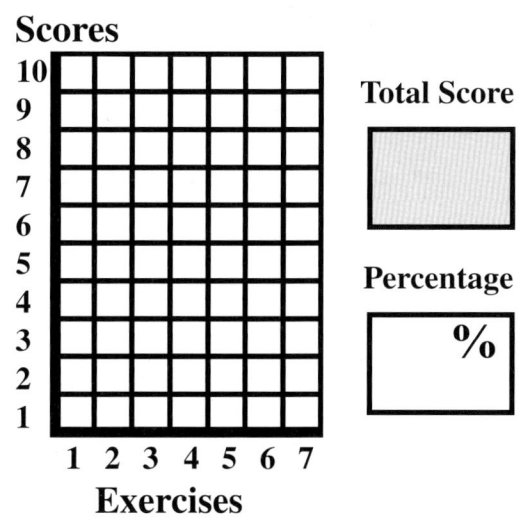

Add up the percentages and divide by 4

Overall Percentage ___ %

© 2012 Stephen Curran

CERTIFICATE OF
ACHIEVEMENT

This certifies

_____

has successfully completed

11+ Verbal Activity
Year 4/5
WORKBOOK 1

Overall percentage score achieved [ ] %

Comment _____

_____

Signed _____
(teacher/parent/guardian)

Date _____